anythink

Snap
books

Drawing Friesians

and Other Beautiful Horses

by Rae Young

CAPSTONE PRESS
a capstone imprint

Snap Books are published by Capstone Press,
1710 Roe Crest Drive, North Mankato, Minnesota 56003
www.capstonepub.com

Library of Congress Cataloging-in-Publication Data
Young, Rae.
  Drawing Friesians and other beautiful horses / by Rae Young ; illustrated by Q2A Media
      pages cm. — (Snap. Drawing horses)
  Summary: "Step-by-step guides show how to draw a variety of horses and ponies"—Provided by publisher.
  ISBN 978-1-4765-3996-6 (library binding)
  ISBN 978-1-4765-6050-2 (eBook PDF)
1. Horses in art—Juvenile literature. 2. Friesian horse—Juvenile literature. 3. Drawing—Technique—Juvenile
literature. I. Q2A Media (Firm), illustrator. II. Title.
  NC783.8.H65Y682 2014c
  743.6'96655—dc23   2013031805

Editorial Credits
Mari Bolte, editor; Lori Bye, designer; Jennifer Walker, production specialist

Photo Credits
All illustrations are by Q2AMedia Services Private Ltd, except for June Brigman, 30-31

Printed in China by Nordica.
1013/CA21301921
092013   007745NORDS14

TABLE OF CONTENTS

GETTING STARTED

Some artists see the world as their canvas. Others see the world as their pasture! If you're a horse lover, grab a pencil and a notebook. Just pick a project and follow the step-by-step instructions. Even if you've never drawn a horse before, the projects in this book will get you started. You'll have everything you need to draw a funny foal or a record-setting racehorse.

Once you've mastered the basics, try giving your art a personal touch. Customize each horse's saddle pad or halter with bright colors and patterns. Add in details like silver conchos or textured leather. Draw accessories such as winter blankets, first-place ribbons, or buckets and brushes. Why not try drawing your friends on a trail ride or galloping across a beach? Don't be afraid to get creative!

TOOLS OF THE TRADE

1. Every artist needs something to draw on. Clean white paper is perfect for creating art. Use a drawing pad or a folder to organize your artwork.

2. Pencils are great for both simple sketches and difficult drawings. Always have one handy!

3. Finish your drawing with color! Colored pencils, markers, or even paints give your equine art detail and realism.

4. Want to add more finishing touches? Try outlining and shading your drawings with artist pens.

5. Don't be afraid of digital art! There are lots of free or inexpensive drawing apps for tablets or smartphones. Apps are a great way to experiment with different tools while on the go.

CURLY CURLS

Like its name suggests, the Bashkir Curly has a curly, poodlelike coat. Even the Bashkir Curly's eyelashes have curls! Its curls are described as long ringlets, deep waves, or soft velvet.

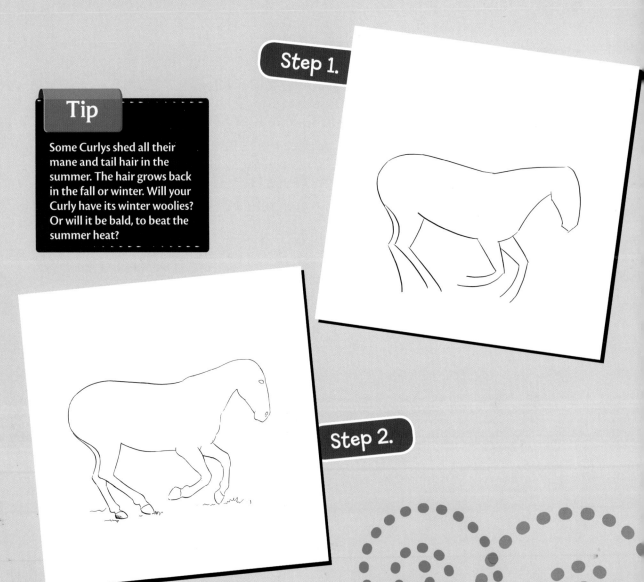

Tip

Some Curlys shed all their mane and tail hair in the summer. The hair grows back in the fall or winter. Will your Curly have its winter woolies? Or will it be bald, to beat the summer heat?

Step 1.

Step 2.

Step 3.

Step 4.

READY TO GO

These horses are in the trailer waiting to head out. Whether they're hauling down the road or driving across the country, these three are ready to go!

Step 1.

Tip

Give each horse an identity! Pick different colors from the rainbow of horse coat colors and patterns. Draw different halter types and colors. Why not stencil each horse's name above its head?

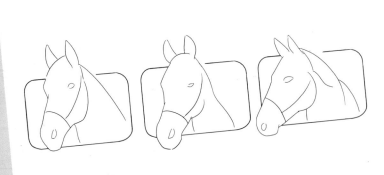

Step 2.

HOIST THE FLAG

Parade horses lead the way during celebrations, rodeos, and horse shows. Parade horses must be dependable and calm. They should also be spirited enough to get the crowd's attention. Decorate your horse with flashy tack, a bright flag, and patriotic paint.

Step 1.

Step 2.

Tip

Cover your fancy parade saddle in traditional silver conchos. You can also add stirrup covers, called tapaderos. Don't forget the drape on the back of the saddle, called a serape.

Step 3.

Step 4.

A TEAM IN MINIATURE

Miniature horses are a good choice for people who don't want to ride but still like to be around horses. Although they are too small to ride, minis excel at driving. They are most commonly driven single, in pairs, or four-in-hand.

Step 1.

Step 2.

Tip

Once you finish drawing this tiny pair, draw two more for a four-in-hand team! Four-in-hand teams are four horses controlled by a single driver.

Step 3.

Step 4.

13

MEDIEVAL MARE

Jet black with long, flowing manes, tails, and leg feathering, Friesians are one of the most recognizable breeds. Used as warhorses in times past, Friesians bring a taste of history to medieval jousts. Add a knight and you're ready to face your foe.

Step 1.

Step 2.

Step 3.

Step 4.

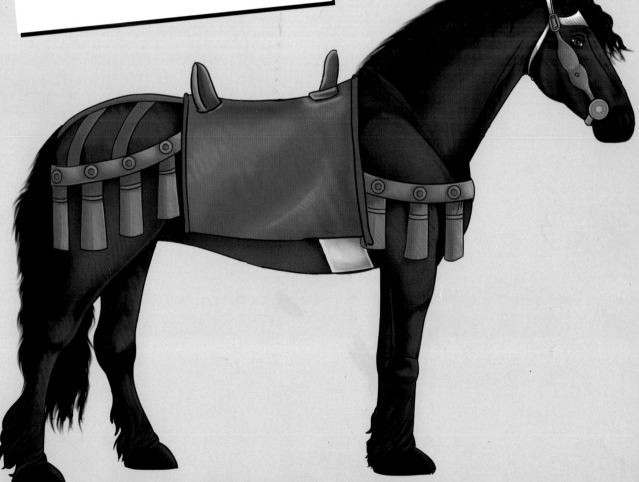

SMALL IN SIZE

Miniature horses usually look like either small stock horses or small Arabians. The type of halter they are shown in reflects that. Draw a stock horse halter made of leather and covered in silver. Or choose a thin, delicate Arabian halter to show off your horse's head.

Step 1.

Tip

When you're done with this horse, why not draw the rest of the class?

Step 2.

Step 3.

Step 4.

PERFECT PIAFFE

The piaffe (PE-aff) is an instant crowd-pleaser. This advanced dressage movement shows off a horse's ability to trot in place. Draw your horse with more of its weight to its hind end. Then you can give its front legs more action.

Tip

Decorate your horse's saddle pad with breed logos, monograms, or country flags. Trim the pad with fleece, ribbon, or piping.

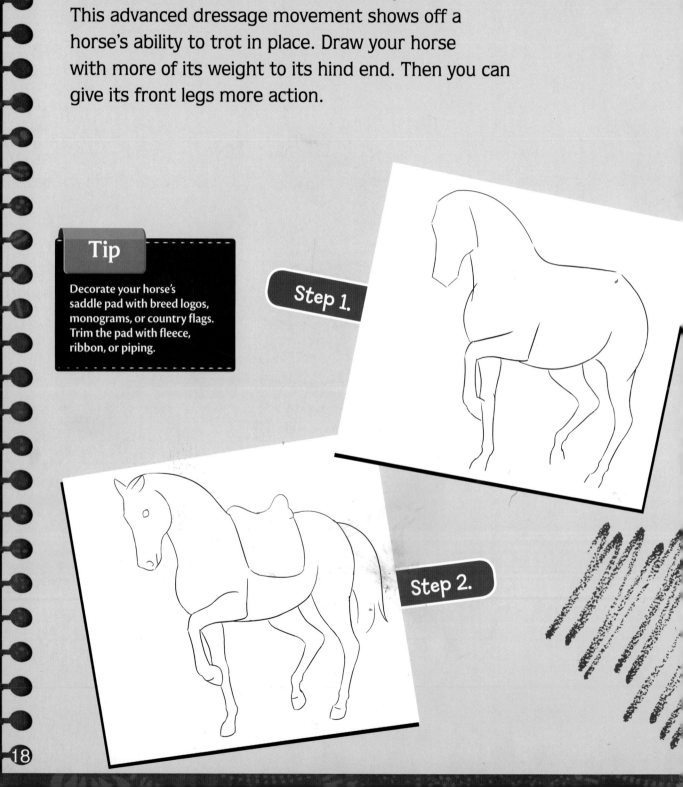

Step 1.

Step 2.

Step 3.

Step 4.

A FUNNY PAIR

Mules are a cross between horses and donkeys. They come in all shapes and sizes, from miniatures under 36 inches (91 cm) to giant drafts. Any breed of horse or pony, including the Welsh pony shown here, can be crossed with a donkey to make a mule.

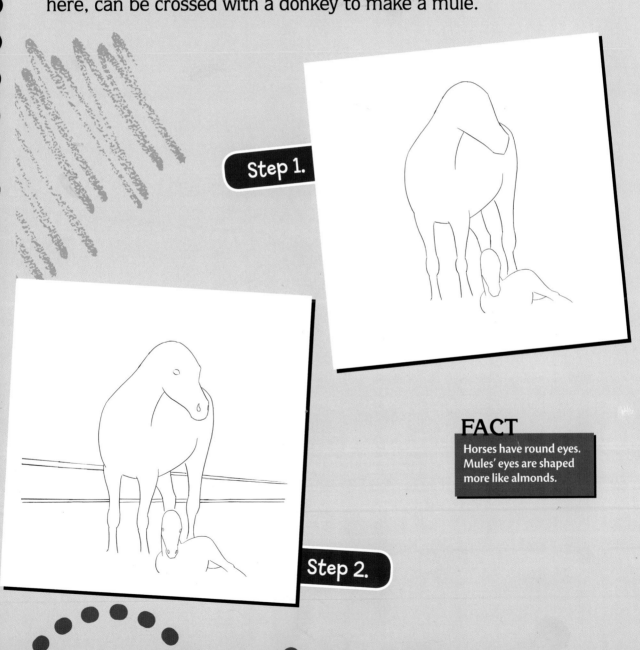

Step 1.

Step 2.

FACT
Horses have round eyes. Mules' eyes are shaped more like almonds.

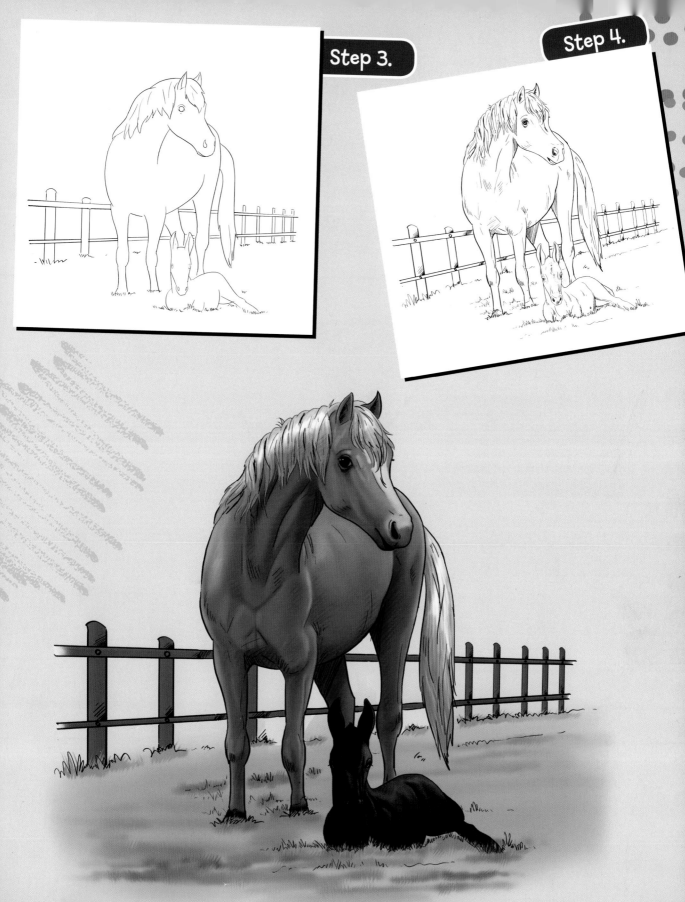

Step 3.

Step 4.

21

SNOWY HORSE

Haflingers are small horses, standing between 12.2 and 14.3 hands high. They are always chestnut colored, with lighter white or flaxen manes and tails. They are heavier horses, weighing between 900 and 1,300 pounds (408 and 590 kilograms). This makes them suitable for both draft work and riding.

Tip

Give your haflinger more winter touches by adding a furry coat and visible breaths of air.

Step 1.

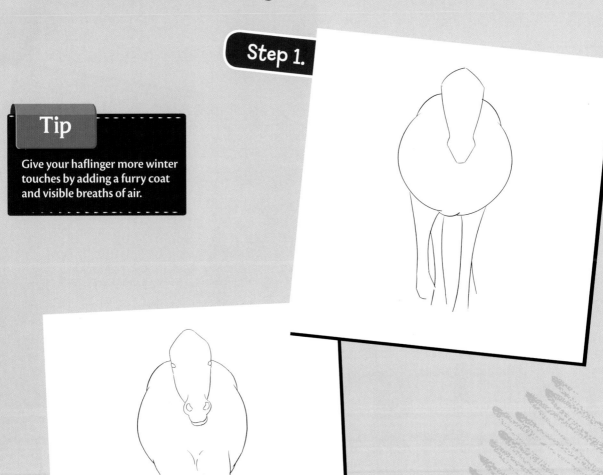

Step 2.

Step 3.

Step 4.

BIG AND LITTLE

Horses of all sizes love to play. Capture the playful spirit of a miniature horse and its full-sized friend as they frolic in the pasture. Dainty ears and hooves and a fluffy coat show off the mini horse's features.

Step 1.

FACT

Only miniature horses and Ponies of the Americas (POAs) are measured in inches. Miniature horses stand under 34 inches (86 cm) tall. Make sure to draw your small friend the right size!

Step 2.

Step 4.

Step 3.

SPLASHED IN PAINT

Paint horses come in any color mixed with white. Their spotted color patterns are called pinto. Experiment by mixing the shape and size of the horse's spots. It's time to get creative!

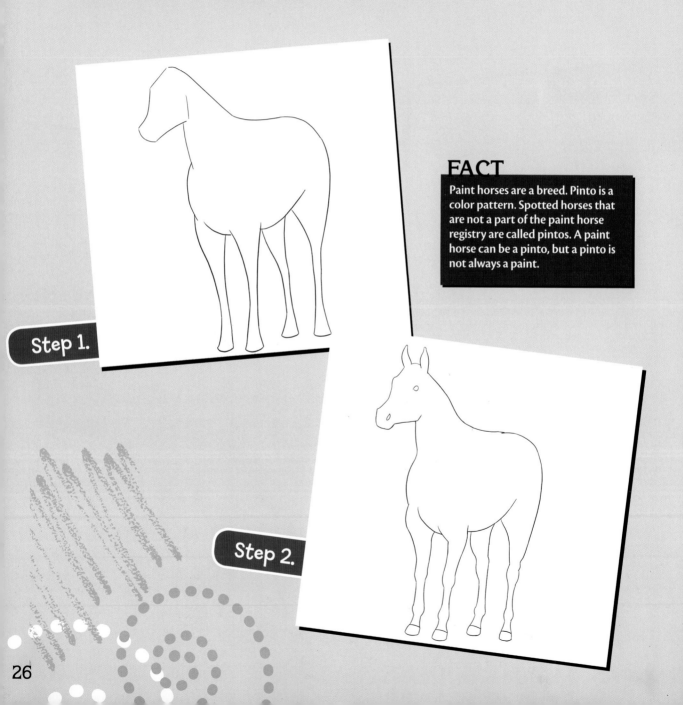

Step 1.

Step 2.

FACT

Paint horses are a breed. Pinto is a color pattern. Spotted horses that are not a part of the paint horse registry are called pintos. A paint horse can be a pinto, but a pinto is not always a paint.

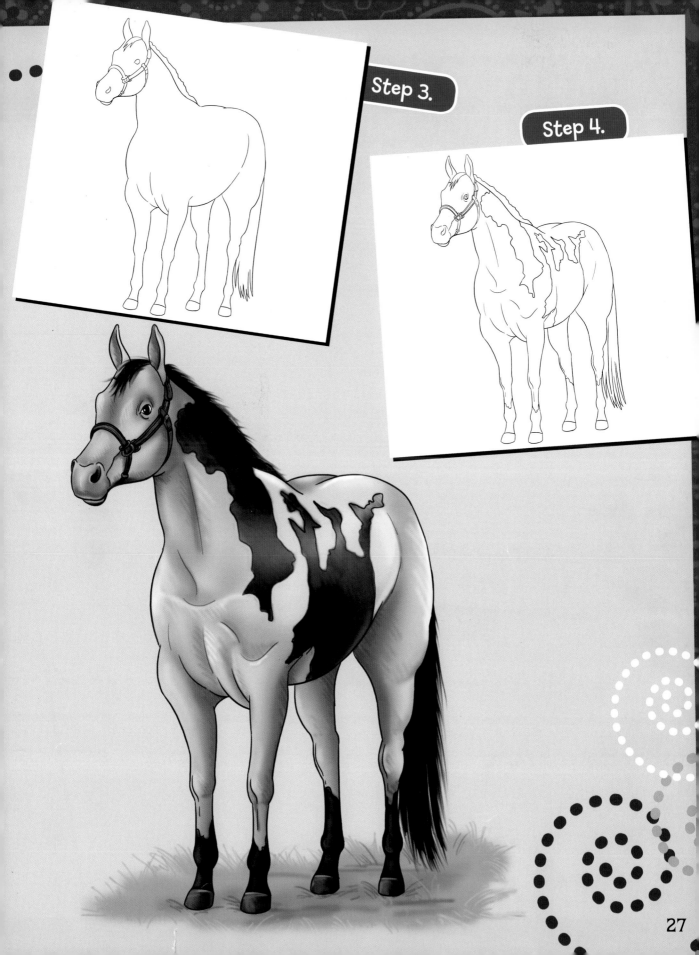

Step 3.

Step 4.

AFTERNOON NAP

A relaxed horse will stand with its head down and ears to the side. Add droopy lips, a cocked hind leg, and closed eyes to your sleepy steed.

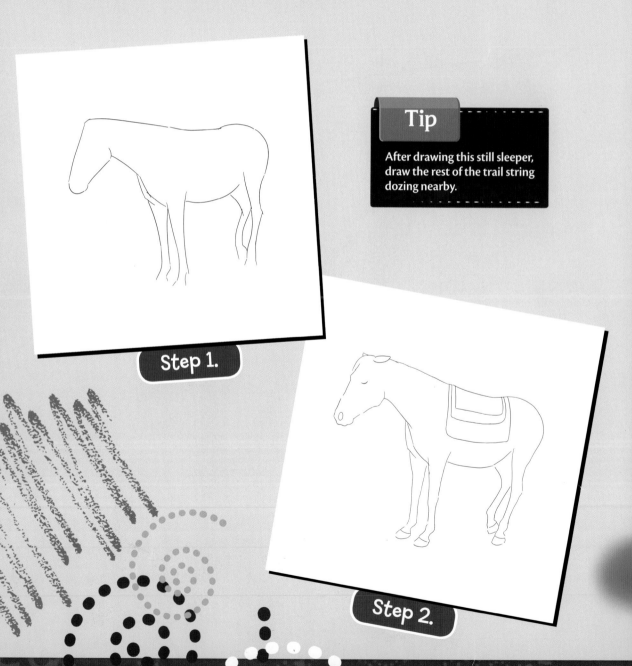

Step 1.

Step 2.

Tip

After drawing this still sleeper, draw the rest of the trail string dozing nearby.

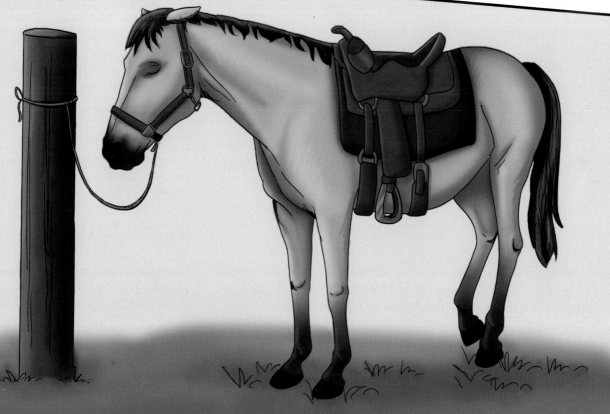

DANCING LIPIZZANER

Lipizzaners are known for their "airs above the ground." These movements are performed with or without a rider. This Lippizaner is performing the courbette. The horse balances on its hind legs, and then jumps straight up in the air.

Step 1.

Step 2.

Tip

Almost all Lipizzaners are gray. They are born bay or black, and turn gray as they mature. Draw a younger Lipizzaner by coloring it a darker shade of gray.

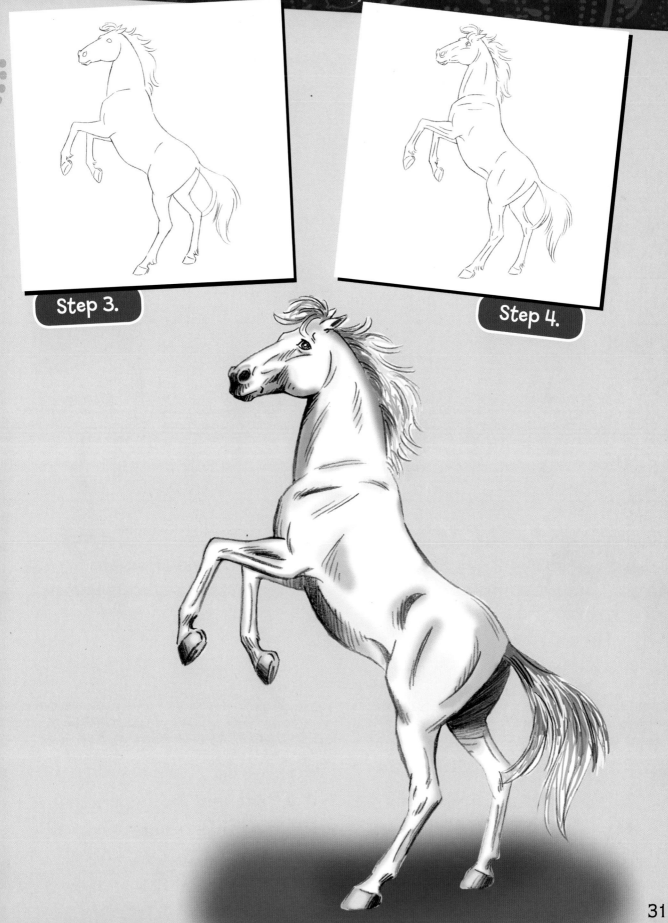

Step 3.

Step 4.

INTERNET SITES

FactHound offers a safe, fun way to find Internet sites related to this book. All of the sites on FactHound have been researched by our staff.

Here's all you do:

Visit *www.facthound.com*

Type in this code: 9781476539966

LOOK FOR ALL THE BOOKS IN THIS SERIES

Drawing Appaloosas and Other Handsome Horses

Drawing Friesians and Other Beautiful Horses

Drawing Arabians and Other Amazing Horses

Drawing Mustangs and Other Wild Horses

Drawing Barrel Racers and Other Speedy Horses

Drawing Thoroughbreds and Other Elegant Horses